MESSAGE INTERCEPT

Woody is listening to the Green Army Men on the baby monitor.
They are telling him about the new toys Andy has gotten for his birthday,
but the message is hard to understand. Help unscramble the message
below by rearranging some of the letters in the words.

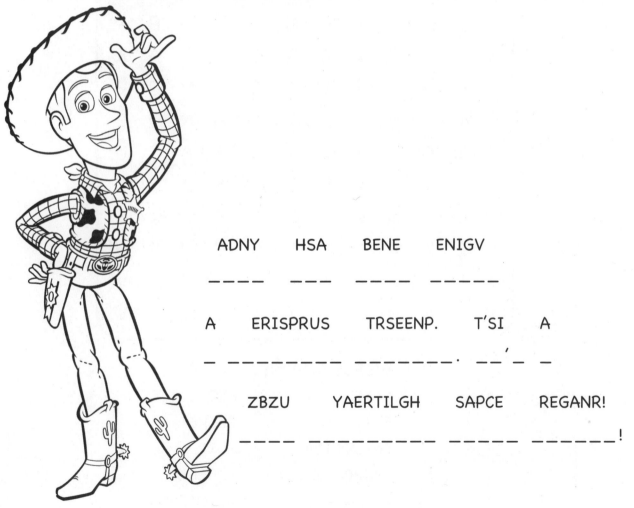

ADNY   HSA   BENE   ENIGV

____ ___ ____ _____

A   ERISPRUS   TRSEENP.   T'SI   A

_ _____ _____. __'_ _

ZBZU   YAERTILGH   SAPCE   REGANR!

____ _____ _____ _____!

Answer: Andy has been given a surprise present. It's a Buzz Lightyear space ranger!

INCREDIBLE SEARCH

There are ten words hiding in the puzzle below. See if you can find them all!

```
F I A D U T H M Y Y L P
E D N P K E M W C P E A
X J M C F R N E P U P P
P R E R R C J O I O A K
L I D T I E S O R M C R
O M K V I S D E A N D E
S I G L P U S I X A O U
I R W J N R S G B J C C
O A B X E L O O J L Q E
N G X P I J J Y C U E U
X E U R A H M O D E A V
M S S D O P I C O L E V
```

WORDS TO FIND:

CAPE   MODE

EDNA   SECRET

EXPLOSION   SUIT

INCREDIBLE   SUPERS

MIRAGE   VELOCIPOD

Answers:

DASH WORDS

Dash is a superfast runner, but he has trouble getting away from the guards on the island.

Use the clues below to find out what the guards are using to keep up with Dash.

The first letter of each answer spells the Secret Word.

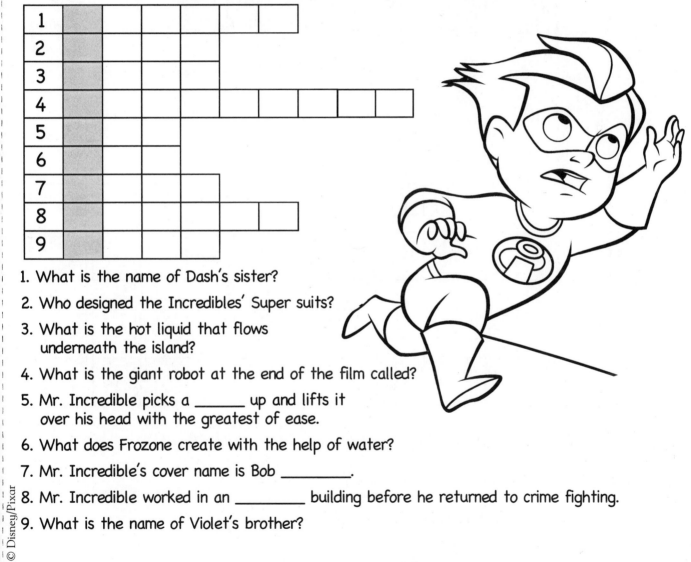

1. What is the name of Dash's sister?

2. Who designed the Incredibles' Super suits?

3. What is the hot liquid that flows underneath the island?

4. What is the giant robot at the end of the film called?

5. Mr. Incredible picks a _____ up and lifts it over his head with the greatest of ease.

6. What does Frozone create with the help of water?

7. Mr. Incredible's cover name is Bob _____.

8. Mr. Incredible worked in an _____ building before he returned to crime fighting.

9. What is the name of Violet's brother?

Answers: 1. Violet 2. Edna 3. Lava 4. Omnidroid 5. Car 6. Ice 7. Parr 8. Office 9. Dash   Secret Word: VELOCIPOD

BYE-BYE, MONSTROPOLIS!

Oh, dear! Waternoose has thrown
Sulley and Mike out of Monstropolis!
Can you help them find their way home?
Decode the message below to introduce
them to a helpful friend.

A	B	C	D	E	F	G	H	I	J	K	L	M
6	21	15	3	10	24	4	18	13	22	1	25	8

N	O	P	Q	R	S	T	U	V	W	X	Y	Z
26	11	23	2	17	14	19	5	9	12	20	16	7

___ ___ ___ ___ ___ ___ ___ ___ ___ ___
 6   21   11   8   13   26   6   21   25   10

___ ___ ___ ___ ___ ___ ___
14   26   11   12   8   6   26

Answer: Abominable Snowman

A MONSTER MYSTERY

Randall has chased Sulley and Mike through Monsters, Inc. Find out where they ended up by crossing out the letters that appear four times or more in the grid. Use the leftover letters to spell out the answer in the space provided.

X	F	B	Q	S
N	D	Q	O	P
F	S	O	Z	K
X	B	K	R	N
V	S	Z	C	S
K	A	N	Q	P
C	P	C	U	X
F	X	L	F	K
C	P	B	T	Z
Z	Q	Z	N	B

__ __ __ __

__ __ __ __ __

Answer: Door vault

HOME, SWEET HOME

Can you help the circus bugs find their way to Flik's home? Decode the message to find the name of the place he lives. Use the clues to help you fill in the puzzle. The first letter of each word spells the Secret Word.

— — — —   — — — — — —

1. Which princess is about to become queen? _ _ _ _ _
2. A bird builds a _ _ _ _ for its babies.
3. The two Hungarian pill bug acrobats are _ _ _ _ and Roll.
4. The fake bird was one of Flik's _ _ _ _ _ _ _ _ _ _ _.
5. What is the name of the walking stick in the movie? _ _ _ _ _
6. What type of bug is Francis? _ _ _ _ _ _ _ _
7. What type of insect is Flik? _ _ _
8. The opposite of day is _ _ _ _ _.
9. Princess Atta's little sister is _ _ _.

Answers: 1. Atta 2. Nest 3. Tuck 4. Inventions 5. Slim 6. Ladybug 7. Ant 8. Night 9. Dot   Secret Word: Ant Island

BUG DECODER

Flik has come up with another amazing invention! Can you decode the secret message below to find out what he has created?

A	B	C	D	E	F	G	H	I	J	K	L	M
6	19	17	13	24	10	22	2	26	25	16	12	5

N	O	P	Q	R	S	T	U	V	W	X	Y	Z
9	14	7	3	23	20	8	15	1	18	4	11	21

___ ___ ___ ___ ___ ___ ___ ___ ___
6   15   8   14   5   6   8   26   17

___ ___ ___ ___ ___ ___ ___ ___ ___
2   6   23   1   24   20   8   24   23

Answer: Automatic harvester

OCEAN PUZZLE

A blue-ringed octopus can change its colors so that it can hide in the ocean. See how many words you can change OCTOPUS into by using the letters to create new words. The first one is done for you:

O C T O P U S

STOP   _____   _____

_____   _____   _____

_____   _____   _____

_____

Some words you might find: cut, pot, scoot, soup, spot, top, us

DORY DECODER

Poor Dory keeps forgetting everything! Help her find something she really needs by crossing out the letters that appear four times or more in the grid. Use the leftover letters to spell out the answer in the space provided.

A	Q	T	C	H
N	M	L	N	J
J	N	Q	X	C
H	J	E	I	L
Q	T	N	A	N
H	M	T	C	I
A	H	J	O	J
X	T	I	L	C
X	R	Q	C	I
X	A	X	Y	L

__ __ __ __ __ __

Answer: Memory

THE SUPERS' WORD SEARCH

There are ten words hiding in the puzzle below. See if you can find them!

```
E P X J M A W I E F I W
K D L I K K S J B F C M
G J Z R D P P E B V R S
S I A V I E H S A D I C
Y E S Z O G N D M C M W
N V C L U L I T S Z E K
D I N I A M C T I I H L
R U U I V N C A S T T E
O O Z G V K D P N A Y O
M F E S R K N G N O L X
E Y J D N A B S U H A E
T Y E F Z K O R X U A E
```

WORDS TO FIND:

CRIME	IDENTITY
DASH	ISLAND
ELASTIGIRL	SYNDROME
HUSBAND	VOLCANO
ICE	WIFE

© Disney/Pixar

EDNA'S CROSSWORD!

ACROSS

3. Mr. Incredible receives a special message in his _____.
5. Mr. Incredible's cover name is _____ Parr.
7. Explosive villain: Bomb _____.
8. Mr. Incredible and Frozone love to _____ crime.

DOWN

1. This cool dude's special power is making ice.
2. The youngest member of the Parr family.
4. She can protect herself with a force field.
6. Elastigirl's cover name is _____ Parr.

Answers: Across: 3. Briefcase 5. Bob 7. Voyage 8. Fight   Down: 1. Frozone 2. Jack-Jack 4. Violet 6. Helen

FIND THE MONSTER

The Child Detection Agency (CDA) is trying to track down Waternoose. Can you help its agents figure out which room he is in? Use the clues to help you fill in the puzzle. The first letter of each answer spells the Secret Word.

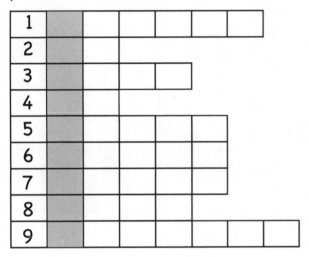

1							
2							
3							
4							
5							
6							
7							
8							
9							

___ ___ ___ ___ ___ ___ ___ ___ ___

1. Which big blue monster is Mike's best friend?
2. The opposite of out is _____.
3. Which monster has a girlfriend named Celia?
4. The opposite of down is _____.
5. Sulley changed the Scare Floor into the _____ Floor.
6. Roz was secretly the CDA's number one _____.
7. A human child is _____ to monsters.
8. The opposite of closed is _____.
9. Which monster has a devilish plan to collect screams from children?

Answers: 1. Sulley 2. In 3. Mike 4. Up 5. Laugh 6. Agent 7. Toxic 8. Open 9. Randall   Secret word: SIMULATOR

MONSTER MAZE

Poor Boo needs to find her way home! Can you help the little girl find her way back to the right bedroom?

Answer: Path B

FUN WITH FLIK

Poor Flik must defeat the grasshoppers, but he can't do it alone! Find out who he gets to help him by crossing out the letters that appear four times in the grid below. Use the leftover letters to spell out the answer in the space provided.

T	W	J	K	O
W	C	Y	Q	Y
O	P	I	P	V
P	W	Q	N	O
K	N	R	C	V
Y	V	J	W	P
J	U	K	S	V
Y	O	T	Q	N
Q	B	T	U	T
G	K	N	J	S

__ __ __ __ __ __

__ __ __ __ __

Answer: Circus bugs

BUG STORY

To finish this story you will need to select the correct words from the leaf and place them in the missing spaces below.

Flik, grasshoppers, right, bugs, harvester, destroyed, City, angry

A creative ant named _____ had invented an amazing automatic

_____. When the time came to show everybody his invention, the

harvester went crazy and _____ all the grain they had

collected.

Everybody was _____ at Flik. He knew he had to make everything

_____ again, so he went to The _____ to find bigger _____ to help defeat

the _____.

Answers: Flik, harvester, destroyed, angry, right, City, bugs, grasshoppers

TOY STORY TALE

To finish this story you will need to select the correct words below and place them in the missing spaces.

window, danger, Buzz Lightyear, Andy's, toy, save

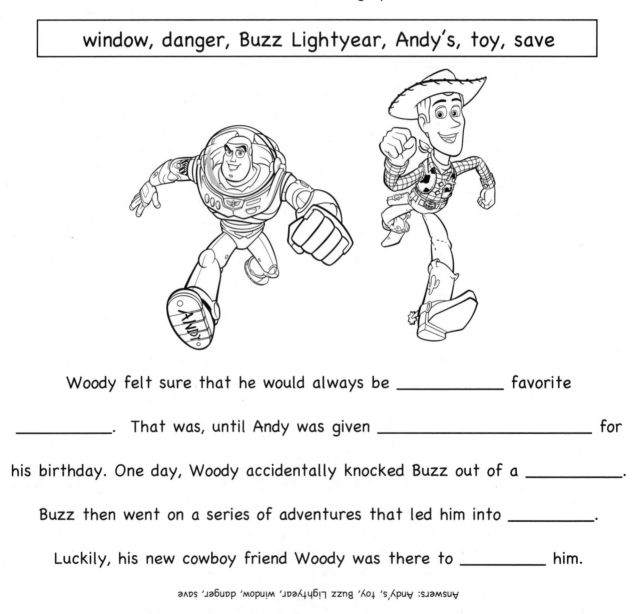

Woody felt sure that he would always be _____ favorite

_____. That was, until Andy was given _____ for

his birthday. One day, Woody accidentally knocked Buzz out of a _____.

Buzz then went on a series of adventures that led him into _____.

Luckily, his new cowboy friend Woody was there to _____ him.

Answers: Andy's, toy, Buzz Lightyear, window, danger, save

MYSTERY MISSION

Buzz Lightyear is on a mission to find his archenemy.
Help Buzz by crossing out the letters that appear four times or more in the grid
below. Write the remaining letters in the spaces provided below.

__ __ __ __ __ __ __

__ __ __ __

X	C	E	C	Y	J
D	D	W	M	Y	Q
A	C	A	Y	A	N
X	P	W	E	V	J
R	L	O	J	N	Y
X	C	X	R	V	B
D	Z	J	V	Q	L
A	W	U	N	N	R
D	V	W	Q	B	B
A	L	B	G	Q	L

© Disney/Pixar

Answer: Emperor Zurg

UNDERWATER CROSSWORD

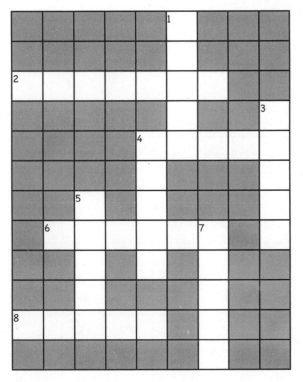

Across
2. A sea animal with eight legs is an _____.
4. Nemo is orange, black, and _____.
6. Nemo's dad is called _____.
8. What type of creature is Bruce?

Down
1. Name of one of the sea turtles.
3. What is the name of the starfish in the fish tank with Nemo?
4. Marlin and Dory were almost swallowed by a huge _____.
5. The dentist's niece who plans to take Nemo home is called _____.
7. What is the name of the pelican who helps Marlin and Dory find Nemo?

© Disney/Pixar

Answers: Across: 2. Octopus 4. White 6. Marlin 8. Shark Down: 1. Crush 3. Peach 4. Whale 5. Darla 7. Nigel

WATERY WORD FIND

Dive in and search for your friends from *Finding Nemo*.
See if you can find 11 names hidden in the puzzle.

U	G	I	L	L	E	C	B
U	E	O	M	S	G	D	E
B	I	E	N	Q	U	O	I
R	B	N	P	U	R	R	R
U	L	E	E	I	G	Y	M
C	O	M	A	R	L	I	N
E	A	O	C	T	E	P	I
C	T	O	H	I	R	R	G
V	Y	X	Z	L	T	T	E
B	C	R	U	S	H	X	L

Words to Find:

Nemo	Bloat
Dory	Squirt
Bruce	Gill
Gurgle	Nigel
Peach	Crush
Marlin	

Answers:

MONSTERS, INC. WORDS

Mike calls his girlfriend, Celia, all sorts of funny names, including Schmoopsie-Poo.
Using the letters of SCHMOOPSIE, see how many words you can make.
The first one is done for you.

S C H M O O P S I E

SCOOP

_____   _____   _____

Some words you might find: come, cop, hip, home, hoop, hope, me, mop, pie, sip, smooch, so

SCARER STORY

To finish this story you will need to select the correct words from around the doorway below and place them in the missing spaces.

Waternoose

Scarer

children

Mike

Sulley

scream

Randall is determined to beat _____ and become

the number one _____ at Monsters, Inc. He has

made a plan with _____ to create a

_____ machine that will steal screams

from _____. Luckily, Sulley and _____

find out and save the day before it's too late!

Answers: Sulley, Scarer, Waternoose, scream, children, Mike

WORDS IN DISGUISE!

Mr. Incredible has received a special communication from a secret contact telling him about a "Super" new job. To find out who has sent him the message, cross out the letters that appear three times in the grid below and arrange the remaining letters to reveal the mystery person.

___ ___ ___ ___ ___ ___

M	X	G	H	X
Q	O	N	C	Q
F	J	F	J	C
D	S	B	J	E
T	B	O	O	H
N	S	R	D	T
L	I	N	C	L
L	X	S	D	T
Q	F	A	H	B

Answer: Mirage

SYNDROME SCRAMBLE!

Mr. Incredible is held captive by the evil Syndrome. Elastigirl flies to the island to rescue him, but her jet is attacked! Realizing Dash and Violet have smuggled themselves onboard, Elastigirl pleads with the control tower to stop firing missiles. In the confusion, her message is scrambled. Can you make sense of what she is saying? Unscramble the message below to find out.

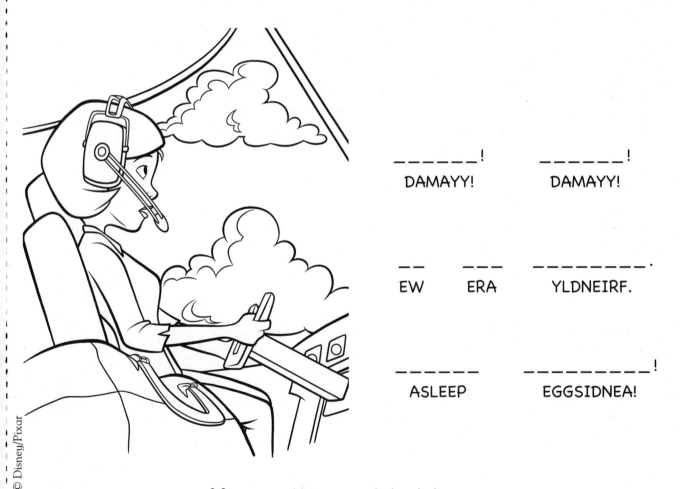

_ _ _ _ _ _ !
DAMAYY!

_ _ _ _ _ _ !
DAMAYY!

_ _   _ _ _   _ _ _ _ _ _ _ _ _ .
EW   ERA   YLDNEIRF.

_ _ _ _ _ _
ASLEEP

_ _ _ _ _ _ _ _ _ !
EGGSIDNEA!

SPACE SEARCH

Buzz Lightyear wants to save the universe from the evil Emperor Zurg.
Help Buzz break the code and rocket through outer space.

A	B	C	D	E	F	G	H	I	J	K	L	M
11	4	24	21	7	1	15	9	26	18	23	5	12

N	O	P	Q	R	S	T	U	V	W	X	Y	Z
16	8	2	25	14	20	10	6	19	3	13	17	22

___ ___   ___ ___ ___ ___ ___ ___ ___ ___
10   8   26   16   1   26   16   26   10   17

___ ___ ___   ___ ___ ___ ___ ___ ___
11   16   21   4   7   17   8   16   21

Answer: To infinity and beyond